Oscar's

Book of Letters

Created by Jane Elizabeth Earley

AuthorHouse™ UK
1663 Liberty Drive
Bloomington, IN 47403 USA
www.authorhouse.co.uk
Phone: 0800.197.4150

Published by AuthorHouse 01/13/2017

ISBN: 978-1-5246-7615-5 (sc)
ISBN: 978-1-5246-7616-2 (e)

Library of Congress Control Number: 2016921626

Print information available on the last page.

This book is printed on acid-free paper.

authorHOUSE®

Drums

Elephant

Ice cream

Ice cream

Kites

Moon

Numbers

1 2 3

4 5

6

> 8

9

Numbers

Oscar

Rabbit
Rabbit
Rabbit
Rabbit

Sandcastles

Teacups

Teacups

Umbrella

Xylophone

Xylophone

yo-yo

Zebra

Zebra

Lightning Source UK Ltd.
Milton Keynes UK
UKRC01n0623130317
296395UK00003B/52